Filling Out
Job Application Forms

Filling Out
Job Application Forms

Library of Congress Cataloging in Publication Data

McHugh, John J
  Filling out job application forms.

  (Practical job skills series)
  SUMMARY: Uses a story line to present the skills neces-
sary in making an application for a job.
  1. Applications for positions. [1. Applications for positions]
I. Stokes, Jim. II. Title. III. Series.
HF5383.M22   650.1'4   80-18255
ISBN O-88436-785-1

Published by EMC Publishing
300 York Avenue
St. Paul, Minnesota
Printed in the United States of America
0 9 8 7 6 5 4 3 2

Filling Out
Job Application Forms

by
John McHugh

Consultants: Dwayne L. Brubaker
Supervisor of Work Experience Education
Los Angeles Unified School District

Maurice E. Wilson, Ed. D.
Director, Dade County Schools
Miami, Florida

Photography by Jim Stokes

Changing Times Education Service • A Division of EMC Publishing
Saint Paul, Minnesota

Acknowledgment

Photographs on pages 18, 20, 21 and 22 were made with the cooperation of Jefferson Lines, Inc., Minneapolis, Minnesota.

Contents

CHAPTER 1
The Man from Chicago

Billy Lee Evans had a secret. He had been keeping it to himself all week. It felt like something heavy weighing him down. It was not a bad secret. Not at all. He was just waiting for the right time to tell it to his mother and his three sisters.

It all began some three weeks before. Billy Lee was working at Lorenzo's Calexico Station in Crocketts. It was one of the places he worked part-time since he graduated from Mountain Ridge High School. It was Saturday night, a busy night at Lorenzo's. More people were using the Interstate Highway then. And Lorenzo's was one of the few gas stations open late near the Interstate.

Billy Lee was friendly to all of the people who came to Lorenzo's. But he especially liked to talk to people who came from places far away from Crocketts. To him, they were like people from another world. They did things and went places he only dreamed about. They even looked and talked differently than the people he knew.

This Saturday night, Billy Lee was talking to a man from Chicago. The man's car had a flat tire. Lorenzo's son Clay was changing it.

"This looks like a real nice town," said the man from Chicago. "I'd like to come back here in the summer. Do you get a lot of people here in the summer?"

"We get some," answered Billy Lee. "They come here for the fishing. There's been a lot of talk about getting more people to come here. Some folks are for it. But other folks are against it. I don't think anything much is going to come of it. Besides, a lot of the mountains are all cut away. You can't see it from here. But they don't look so nice."

"That's right," said the man from Chicago. "This is a big coal mining area."

"It *was* a big coal mining area," said Billy Lee. "There's not much mining going on now. Just some men digging on their own here and there. The last company mine closed down three years ago."

"Is that right?" said the man. "Well, I suppose that had to hurt. Is there any other industry around here? I see lots of trees on your hills. Do you have a paper industry?"

"No," answered Billy Lee. "The best trees have already been cut away. There was a paper company here. But it closed a while back too."

"Well, what do people do to make a living here?" asked the man.

Billy Lee knew that the man was just making small talk. But he didn't especially like the questions he was asking. The truth was, there were not many ways to make a living in Crocketts any more. The truth was, folks were really hurting.

"Work is hard to find," Billy Lee said. "But folks seem to make out. Lots of people have moved away, though. They go North looking for work. Some even go out West or to Florida."

"That makes sense," said the man. "You have to go where the jobs are. Too bad. This is a pretty town. . . . I guess you're doing all right, though. You must get a lot of business here from the Interstate. Does your dad own this station?"

Billy Lee smiled. "No," he answered. "Clay there, the guy working on your tire, is Lorenzo's son. I just work here when they need help. I've got other jobs, too. I work a few hours a week in a food store. And I help out cleaning up at another store."

"That doesn't sound like much of a life for a boy like you," said the man. "Did you finish high school?"

"Yes, I did," answered Billy Lee. "But it doesn't seem to matter much. I'm lucky to have the part-time jobs I've got. Lots of others don't have anything."

"Why don't you move somewhere else and get a job?" said the man. "A kid like you should be able to get a good job in no time at all. I see ads in the newspaper all the time. They are hungry for people. Say, wait a minute!"

The man went over to his car. He opened the door and took a newspaper from the back seat. He came back to Billy Lee waving the paper in his hand. "Take a look at this!" he said. He opened the newspaper to the Help Wanted ads and held it up to Billy Lee. "See!" he said. "There are hundreds of jobs in the newspaper every day in Chicago."

Billy Lee took the newspaper the man handed him. He ran his eyes quickly over the Help Wanted ads. . . . Yes, the man was right. There were pages and pages of Help Wanted ads. Billy Lee had never seen the Help Wanted ads of a big city newspaper before. He was surprised.

"Keep the paper," said the man. "Read it over when you get time."

Clay had come over to them. He had changed the man's tire and was bringing him the bill. The man took his bill and headed toward the office.

"Thank you for the newspaper," said Billy Lee. "I just might do what you say. I need to make more money. That's for sure."

"Be smart, kid," said the man as he walked away. "Go to Chicago—or any place there are jobs. Give yourself a chance."

"Yes," Billy Lee thought to himself. "Give myself a chance. Go to a place where I can get a good job." The gas station got busy again. He didn't have time to think about it that night.

Sunday afternoon, Billy Lee took the Chicago newspaper with him to a big rock next to Little Muddy Creek. It was the place he went when he wanted to be alone. Wind and water had cut a hole in the top of the rock. Billy Lee could sit in the hole and not be seen by anyone. He spread out the newspaper Help Wanted ads and began to read.

It took him almost an hour to read through all of the ads. Then he went back over them again. This time, he marked off the ads he was interested in with a pen.

His second time through, he saw that most of the jobs that interested him were jobs he could not get. They called for experience or training that he didn't have. And a lot of them wanted people who had gone to college.

He was discouraged. It had all been so exciting. For the first time since leaving Mountain Ridge High School he had felt there was some hope. But now he saw that he had only been dreaming. He had no experience for these Chicago jobs. He hadn't been trained to do anything. And he sure hadn't been to any college.

Billy Lee lay on his back and looked up at the clouding sky. He was feeling sorry for himself. And it wasn't for the first time in his life. He had felt sorry for himself when his

father died eight years ago. He felt sorry for himself when he had to drop off the track team because of his jobs. He felt sorry for himself when he didn't have the money to go on the class trip to Washington, D.C. Most of all, he'd been feeling sorry for himself for not being able to get a full-time job in Crocketts.

Some kids had families with money. They had jobs waiting for them when they graduated from high school. Other kids had gone away to college. Even some poor folks had land they could farm, something to be proud of.

Suddenly the clouds parted and the sun shined brightly. A bird flew over the rock. Surprised to find Billy Lee there, she dropped the worm she was carrying. It fell on the Chicago newspaper.

At first, the worm didn't move at all. Then it began wriggling. Billy Lee sat up and watched the worm wriggle its way off the paper to the rock. He smiled as it went up the side of the rock and disappeared.

Sighing, Billy Lee picked up the newspaper again. This time, he circled the ads for jobs he thought he'd have a chance to get. When he had finished, he didn't feel so bad after all. There were at least ten jobs he could find out about. "And," he told himself, "I *will* find out about them. I've got to get a job. And Chicago is as good a place as any to start looking."

CHAPTER 2
The Secret

Billy Lee Evans is tall and thin. He has red hair and blue eyes. At 19, he is the oldest in his family. His sister Sharon is 14. The twins, Nancy and Nina, are 12.

The Evans family lives in an old house just outside Crocketts. There used to be a farm with the house. But that was sold off years ago while Billy Lee's father was still living. Now even the house is owned by the bank. That happened the winter that Emily Evans, Billy Lee's mother, broke her leg. She could not work, so she had to borrow money on the house.

The whole family depends on what Emily Evans brings in as a waitress. The $40 a week that Billy Lee makes helps a little. They don't have a lot to live on. But they are a happy, loving family.

Billy Lee hated the thought of leaving his mother and sisters. And if things were different, he would never leave Crocketts. His family, the Evans and the Lees, have lived in the Crocketts hill country for about 150 years.

He knew his mother wouldn't like the idea of his leaving, either. He remembered what she said about others who had moved away. There was the time the Allen boys had gone to work in Detroit. They got good jobs in a car assembly plant. But Emily Evans had said, "Those boys are making a big mistake leaving the farm their father left them. They will be sorry later."

And there was the time that Amy Beth Horsley took a job in Pittsburgh. "She was doing all right working in the County Clinic," said Emily Evans. "I can't see why she had to run off all the way to Pittsburgh."

There were others, too. Many younger people had been leaving Crocketts, especially after the mines closed. So Billy Lee knew the way his mother looked at it. At least he thought he did. That's why he was keeping his secret bottled up inside him. He had to find the right time to tell her. And it had to be soon.

Billy Lee answered ten Help Wanted ads from the Chicago newspaper. For two weeks, he surprised his sisters by offering to pick up the mail at the Post Office. And every day of those two weeks, his knees would shake as he checked the box at the Post Office.

He got four letters saying that the jobs had been filled. He got three letters saying that he didn't have the right experience or training. Two places never answered him at all. But the letter that counted, the letter he had hoped for, was the last letter he got. This was the letter that would start him on his way to Chicago. And that was the secret that had been weighing him down all week.

This is the Help Wanted ad Billy Lee answered that brought him the letter.

I need someone to learn my business. Are you young and strong? Are you willing to learn? If you are a high school graduate and want to get in on the ground floor, I'll teach you how to run my business. You don't need experience. I'll train you how to do things my way. Write a letter telling me about yourself. A. Grimes, Box 3438, Chicago Bulletin. Only those willing to work hard need apply!

Billy Lee had answered the ad in the office at Lorenzo's Calexico Station along with the other ads. He had liked it better than the other ads. It sounded more open and honest. But he had expected to find out what kind of business A. Grimes was running when he answered his letter. Instead, there was just this short note.

2343 Stockyard Boulevard
Chicago, Illinois 60600

Dear Billy,

I liked your letter. You sound like the kind of person I have been looking for. The job is yours if you want it. But I'd like to meet you just to make sure you don't have two heads or something like that. Two weeks should be enough time for you to settle things at home and get to Chicago. I'll see you then.

A. Grimes

It had taken Billy Lee all week to get ready to go to Chicago. He had to get the money Lorenzo owed him for working. He had to use that and some of the money he had saved to buy a bus ticket and some new clothes. He had the ticket and the clothes now. He was planning to leave on Monday. Tonight, Sunday, he was going to tell his mother and sisters that he had a job in Chicago and was leaving in the morning.

They were at the dinner table, the five of them and Emily Evans' friend Jeff Stanton. Billy Lee waited until they were almost finished eating to tell them his secret. But everyone knew that something was up. He'd been acting strangely all week. And tonight he had hardly touched his dinner.

Everyone stopped talking when Billy Lee spoke. They were all wondering what he was going to say. "Momma," he said. "I've got something to tell you. I hope it won't make you mad."

"I knew you had something on your mind," said Emily Evans. "What's wrong?"

"Nothing is wrong!" said Billy Lee. "It's just that I don't think you're going to like what I'm going to do. You see, Momma, I only get a few hours work from Lorenzo. And those other jobs I have don't mean anything. I —"

"Did Lorenzo fire you? I told you that you were spending too much time talking to folks down there!" said Mrs. Evans.

"Give the boy a chance to say what's on his mind, Emily," said Jeff Stanton.

Billy Lee took a deep breath. "Momma," he said, "I'm taking another job. And it's . . . it's in Chicago."

"Chicago!" cried Nancy and Nina, almost in one voice. "Brother is going to Chicago! Can we visit you there, Billy Lee?"

"Chicago!" cried Emily Evans. "Chicago! Well, if that doesn't take the cake. When did all this happen?"

Billy Lee felt better now that his secret was out in the open. His mother looked surprised. But she didn't look mad. "Last week," he answered. "Well, it started about three weeks ago. I wrote in about an ad for a job in the Chicago newspaper. A man gave it to me at the gas station. . . . Look, Momma, you know that there are no jobs for anyone in Crocketts. I've got to go where I can get a real job."

"Yes, Billy Lee, I know," said Emily Evans. "I guess I'm really not all that surprised. I've been thinking you might decide to leave one of these days." She sighed. "Maybe it's the only thing to do. I only wish . . . if we still had the farm."

"It's a smart move, Billy Lee," said Jeff Stanton. "I'd be gone from here in a minute if I didn't have my job with the trucking company. A fellow has to get himself a job that pays something."

"What kind of job is it?" asked Sharon.

"Well," said Billy Lee, "I can't exactly say. It's a training job to help some man run his business. Here, I'll show you all I have on it." He gave the Help Wanted ad and the letter from A. Grimes to his mother.

Mrs. Evans read them and passed them to Sharon. "That's not much to go on, son," she said. "He doesn't say what the job is or how much it pays. What happens if you get there and you don't like it?"

"That's a chance I'll have to take," said Billy Lee. "My mind is made up. I already bought my bus ticket. I'm leaving tomorrow morning."

"So soon!" said his mother. "How about money? How are you going to live until you get paid?"

"I have $285," answered Billy Lee. "It's the money I've been saving. And I sold Clay my hunting rifle. That should last me until I get paid."

"I've got family in Chicago," said Jeff Stanton. "Cousin Lester and his wife live there. They would probably give you room and board until you get on your feet. I'll call Lester tonight long distance."

"Thanks, Jeff," said Billy Lee. He looked at his mother. "Then it's all settled?" He smiled.

Emily Evans looked at him, trying to smile. "Yes, I guess it's all settled. But we are going to miss you, Billy Lee."

"Oh, Billy Lee," said Sharon. She put her arms around n, tears coming to her eyes.

The twins got up and crowded around him. "Can we go see you off on the bus?" asked Nancy. "Will you let us ne visit you real soon?" asked Nina.

"Sure, sure," said Billy Lee. He, too, was fighting back tears.

CHAPTER 3
Getting There

It is a long way from Crocketts to Chicago. For the first few hours on the bus, Billy Lee looked out the window. But by early afternoon he fell asleep. He woke up now and then when the bus stopped to let people on or off. But he didn't talk to anyone until the bus stopped in Indianapolis that night.

"Is anyone sitting here?" someone asked, tapping Billy Lee on the back. Billy Lee turned around and saw a boy pointing to the empty seat next to him.

"No," said Billy Lee. He rubbed the sleep from his eyes. "No one has been sitting there all day. Where are we?"

"Indianapolis," answered the boy. He put his bag overhead and sat down. "How far are you going?"

"Chicago," answered Billy Lee. And he tried to make it sound as though he went to Chicago every day.

"Me too," said the boy. "My name is Rick. What's yours?"

"Billy Lee. Pleased to meet you."

The two boys shook hands.

"Are you from Indianapolis?" asked Billy Lee.

"No," answered Rick. "I had to change buses here. I come from Santo Christo, a long way from here."

"I thought you talked a little different," said Billy Lee. "What country is Santo Christo in?"

Rick laughed. "Santo Christo is in Texas," he said. "But my people have lived there since before it was even Texas—about 300 years." He laughed again. "Down in Santo Christo they would say it was you who talked a little different."

Billy Lee laughed too. "Well what are you doing way up here?" he asked.

"Looking for work," said Rick. "Down in Santo Christo there are too many people and not enough jobs. And most of the jobs are working in the fields picking vegetables and fruit. I want something better. I hear Chicago is a good place to get a job. So here I am, on the way to Chicago."

"I have a job waiting for me in Chicago," said Billy Lee. "The town I come from is seeing hard times too. You know anyone in Chicago?"

"No," answered Rick. "I figure I'll get myself a room somewhere. I don't care about that. It's a job I need."

"What kind of job are you looking for?" asked Billy Lee.

Rick smiled. "Oh, I'm not too choosey. Some place where they don't give you a hassle. I don't like those places where they make you fill out all those papers."

"Papers? What kind of papers?" asked Billy Lee.

"You know, job application forms," said Rick, "They always want you to fill a form out. And some people want to give you tests. I don't like all that hassle, man."

"I've never seen a job application form," said Billy Lee. "I never had to fill one out for the jobs I've had."

20

"Then you're lucky," said Rick. "I don't understand half the things they ask you on them. I used to try to fill them out. But now I just say 'no thanks' and walk out."

"Are the forms hard to read?" asked Billy Lee. "Seems to me that if you do one once, you could just do all the others the same way."

"But they are not all the same!" said Rick. "I never saw two exactly the same. Every company has its own job application form."

"So they *are* hard to read," said Billy Lee.

"Well, maybe they won't be for you," said Rick. "But they are for me. You'll see with that job of yours. They will probably make you fill out a job application form before you start working."

Billy Lee looked a little worried. "The man didn't say anything about an application form when he wrote to me. But then, he didn't say much of anything."

"Well, you'll see," said Rick.

The driver of the bus put out the overhead lights. It was quiet on the bus. Most of the people were asleep by now. Neither Rick nor Billy Lee said anything else the rest of the night.

The sun was coming up when they pulled into the bus station in Chicago. Billy Lee didn't sleep much the last few hours. He was too excited. He had never been so far away from home before. And he'd never been alone in such a big place as Chicago. When the bus stopped, he said to Rick, "I don't have any friends here. And neither do you. Why don't we get together some time? I'm staying with some people from my home town. Where will I be able to find you?"

"I'll be staying at the Decatur YMCA for a few nights," answered Rick. "When I find a job, I'll get a place near where I work. You can ask for me at the Y. Ricardo Rodriguez is my full name."

"Mine is Billy Lee Evans," said Billy Lee as they got off the bus. "I'm supposed to meet this fellow and his wife in the waiting room. Good luck to you! I'll be around to see you!"

They shook hands. Then Rick was lost in the crowd of people leaving the station. Billy Lee waited to get his suitcase. He carried it with him into the waiting room and began looking for the Stantons.

An hour later, he was still looking for the Stantons. The station was busy with people going to and from buses. Billy Lee sat and watched them. At last, a man in work clothes came over to him. "Are you Billy Lee Evans?" he asked.

Billy Lee jumped to his feet. "Yes! Are you Lester Stanton?" he said. He put out his hand. But Lester Stanton didn't shake hands. He seemed troubled. And he was looking down at his feet.

"Look, Billy Lee," said Lester Stanton. "I'm kind of in a hurry. I'm late for work."

Billy Lee picked up his suitcase. "I'm ready to go," he said.

"No, no" said Lester Stanton, looking away. "It's this way. Me and my old lady had a fight. Truth is, she was against it from the start, having you stay with us. I'd do anything for Cousin Jeff. But . . . you see how it is." He turned and looked at Billy Lee. But he could not look him in the eye. "My wife said she would leave me. You're going to have to find some place else to stay."

Billy Lee put his suitcase down. He didn't know what to say.

"Here is $20," said Lester Stanton. He put two bills into Billy Lee's hand. "You should be able to find a good room somewhere. . . . Look, I've got to go now. I'm late for work." With that, he turned and hurried away through the crowded waiting room.

"Thanks," said Billy Lee. But Lester Stanton was gone by then. "Thanks for nothing!" said Billy Lee to himself. He sat down. He needed time to think about what he would do next.

CHAPTER 4
Meeting A. Grimes

It was ten in the morning by the time Billy Lee found his way to 2343 Stockyard Boulevard. He had left his suitcase in a locker at the bus station. Then he had breakfast. He remembered what Rick said about finding a place to live near where you worked. So he had decided to go and see A. Grimes first. Maybe Mr. Grimes could tell him where to find a room near his business.

Finding Stockyard Boulevard had not been easy. He had to ask directions several times. But the Chicago bus drivers were friendly. They told him which buses to take and where to get off and change. But now that he stood outside 2343 Stockyard Boulevard, he wondered if there had been some kind of mistake.

The building was an old apartment house. It was very run down. Many of its windows were boarded up. Some of the other buildings on the street were being torn down.

"Maybe Mr. Grimes' business has something to do with tearing down buildings," thought Billy Lee. "I don't see anything that looks like a factory, a store, or an office." He walked into the building.

There were mailboxes and a row of buzzers just inside the first door. The covers of the mailboxes had all been torn off. And there were no names next to the buzzers. But painted in big red letters was the name "A. Grimes." A red arrow pointed to one of the buzzers. Billy Lee pushed the buzzer. It was for Apartment 320.

"Mr. Grimes must keep some kind of office here while the buildings are being torn down," thought Billy Lee. He pushed the buzzer again. There was no answer. He tried the inside door. It was open. He went in and started climbing the stairs.

Apartment 320 was three floors up. The floors he passed looked like something out of a bad dream. The halls were covered with garbage. Doors had been taken away or were hanging in broken pieces. Pipes had been bent into strange shapes. And it was dark on the stairs. He could hardly see where he was going.

Every now and then, he heard things moving around in the piles of garbage. It sounded like rabbits in the brush back home. But he didn't stop to think what rabbits would be doing in a place like this.

When he reached Apartment 320, he found another large, red "A. Grimes" painted on the door. He knocked. There were noises on the other side. It sounded like cats crying. Then he heard the sound of feet coming to the door.

"Who is it?" called a high, thin voice.

"I'm looking for Mr. Grimes!" he answered. "My name is Billy Lee Evans. I'm supposed to work for Mr. Grimes. Do you know where I can find him?"

There was a noise that sounded like chains being moved. Then there was the sound of sliding bolts. The door opened slowly on an old and very strange looking woman.

"You're looking for *Mister* Grimes?" asked the old woman. "There is no *Mister* Grimes. I'm Annie Grimes. And I'm the one who told you to come to see me about a job, young man."

Billy Lee's mouth fell open. He felt a little sick. This old woman was A. Grimes?

"Well, come in if you're coming!" cried Annie Grimes. "And take care you don't step on any of my little darlings." Three or four large cats were winding their way around and around her feet.

Billy Lee walked into the room, trying to get his thoughts together. The smell of cats and garbage made him want to hold his nose. He looked around the room. The place looked as though it hadn't been cleaned in 50 years!

"Sit down over there somewhere," said Annie Grimes. She pointed to a broken-down couch.

Billy Lee decided to stay where he was. "If you're A. Grimes," he asked, "what is this job all about?"

"Just a minute, young man," said Annie Grimes. "I'm the employer. I'll run this job interview, if you don't mind!"

"Job interview!" cried Billy Lee. "You already hired me for a job, remember? You sent me a letter almost two weeks ago. Now I want to know what this job is, if there *is* a job." He was getting madder every minute.

"Well," said Annie Grimes. "I can see you're not the kind of young man I thought you were. I thought a nice young boy from a farm . . ."

"I'm not from a farm," said Billy Lee. "And I want to know what's going on here."

"I sent out many letters to young people," answered Annie Grimes. She picked up a cat. "That's how I get people in for interviews. . . . And now I can see that you won't do at all. No, you just won't do."

"Do what?" cried Billy Lee.

"Why, learn my business and help me to run it," she answered. "You see these little darlings?" She waved a hand toward the cats in different positions around the room. "I run a cat care service. There must be hundreds of them in other parts of the building. I've lost track."

A strange light came into her eyes as she talked. "You see, many people are not able to keep their little friends. They may be moving to a place where they can't keep pets. Or maybe they live with someone who doesn't like cats. Oh, yes—there *are* people like that! . . . Sometimes their cats have kittens they can't get friends to take. Now, in cases like this, many people don't want to have their cats put to sleep. So they come to me. Everyone knows about me. They call me 'The Cat Lady of Stockyard Boulevard.' For a few dollars, I take them all in. I never put a cat to sleep. They live out their days in perfect happiness. It's my business, so to speak."

"*That's* your business!" cried Billy Lee. "And you expected me to—"

"To care for the cats, of course," said Annie Grimes. "But I don't think you will do. No, I don't think you will do at all. I know you will be very disappointed, but . . ."

Billy Lee had heard enough. He hurried out the door while Annie Grimes was still talking. And he tried to hold his breath until he reached the street.

"The Cat Lady of Stockyard Boulevard!" he said out loud. "I've really done myself proud! My first day in Chicago and I have no job and no place to live. It's a good thing I bought a round-trip bus ticket."

CHAPTER 5
Howard Plummer

Billy Lee was heading back to the bus station. He had to change buses three times. The second change was in a busy shopping area. It was a nice sunny day. And he was in no hurry. He decided to see what Chicago looked like.

At first, the crowds of people moving so quickly along the streets bothered him. So did the noise of the traffic. And he looked up at so many tall buildings that his neck began to hurt. He walked for over an hour, excited by the sights and sounds of the city. He began to feel the magic of the place. If only there was something, some place . . .

He reached a busy corner outside a large department store. Waiting to go across the street, he spotted this sign in the store's window.

LUDERBACH'S IS NOW TAKING APPLICATIONS
FOR THE FOLLOWING POSITIONS

SALESCLERKS
CLERK-TYPISTS
STOCK CLERKS
CUSTODIAL WORKERS

SEE THE PERSONNEL DEPARTMENT
ON THE FOURTH FLOOR

"That's it!" thought Billy Lee. "I'll go in there and apply for a job. I don't want to go back to Crocketts like this."

He made his way into the store and found the elevators. Then he took an elevator to the fourth floor. This floor was all offices. Soon he found a door marked "Personnel." He opened the door and entered a large and very busy waiting room. There was a counter at the far end of the room. A woman was sitting behind it. People were waiting in line to see her.

Billy Lee got into the line. "Is this where you apply for a job?" he asked the young man in front of him.

"Must be," answered the young man. "I just got here myself. I don't see any place else to go. What kind of job are you applying for?"

"I don't know," said Billy Lee. "I'll take anything, I guess. I'm not a typist, though."

"That leaves salesclerk, stock clerk, and custodial," said the young man. "You should choose one of them. Take it from me, these personnel people like it better when you have just one job in mind. Don't know why, but they do. Tell them you want to be a stock clerk. That's what I'm telling them."

"All right," said Billy Lee. "And thanks. I've never applied for a job in a place like this before."

"Well, you're looking at an expert in applying for jobs," said the young man. "I must have applied at just about every place in town. I even dream about filling out job application forms. Bad dreams."

Billy Lee remembered his talk on the bus with Rick Rodriguez about job application forms. Now here it was again. "Do you have trouble filling out job application forms?" he asked.

"No, I don't have trouble filling them out," said the young man. "I have trouble with what I fill them out *with*. Do you dig?"

Billy Lee smiled in answer to the young man's smile. "Yes," he said. But he didn't really know what the young man was talking about. He had no time to ask, either. The young man was talking now to the woman behind the counter.

"Have you applied here before?" she asked him.

"No," the young man answered.

"Which position are you interested in?" she asked.

"Stock clerk," he answered.

"Do you have any experience?" she asked.

"Oh, sure," he answered.

"Well then, fill out this application form and return it to me," she said.

"Thank you," he said. He took the application form and went to one of the long tables on the other side of the room.

Then it was Billy Lee's turn.

"Hello," he said. "I'd like to apply for a job as a stock clerk."

"All right," said the woman. "Do you have any experience?"

"I worked in a store in Crocketts," answered Billy Lee.

The woman looked up at him. She was going to say something. But she didn't. She smiled. Then she handed Billy Lee an application form. "We expect to have openings for several stock clerks," she said. "You can fill out the form at one of the tables over there. Bring it to me when you're finished."

Billy Lee went to the same table the young man had gone to. He sat down next to him and read the job application form.

Trouble popped up in big black letters on the second line. "Present Address"—he had no present address! It wouldn't do any good to put down his Crocketts address, either. They also wanted to know his telephone number. Of course they needed his address and telephone number! How else could they reach him about a job? Billy Lee put the form down on the table and sighed.

The young man next to him looked up from his own application form. "Are you having trouble?" he asked. "I told you that I'm an expert on these things. Just ask old Howard Z. Plummer. What's your problem?"

"I . . . I . . . You see, I just got into town today," said Billy Lee. "I don't have a place to stay. There's nothing I can put down here for 'Present Address.' I have no telephone number to give, either."

"I see," said Howard. He thought for a minute. "Don't you have any idea where you are going to stay? Were you just passing through for the day?"

"I hadn't thought about it," said Billy Lee. "I'd like to stay in Chicago. But I need a job. I was supposed to have a job waiting for me, but —"

"Tell you what," said Howard. "Put down the Decatur YMCA. It's at 530 Decatur Avenue. The telephone number is 543-9800. If you're going to stick around, it's as good a place as any."

"How come you know the telephone number?" asked Billy Lee.

"That's an easy one," answered Howard. "I've been staying there for the last month."

"I thought you were from Chicago," said Billy Lee.

"Good," said Howard. "I'm glad to hear that. I've been working on my accent. Trying to sound like the folks who live here." He laughed. "You see, mon," he went on, "I be cummin from the islands."

"The islands? Which islands?" asked Billy Lee.

"I'm from Marimba, British West Indies," said Howard. "That's in the Caribbean."

"What are you doing way up here in Chicago?" asked Billy Lee.

"Same as you," said Howard, "looking for work. Marimba is a beautiful place. But a person's got to eat. There are no jobs to speak of at home. I've come to the U.S.A. to make my fortune."

"As a stock clerk?"

"Just a beginning, my friend. Remember, big palm trees from little coconuts do grow. Say, what is your name?"

"Billy Lee Evans."

"Nice to meet you," said Howard. "Now go on and fill out your job application form. Later I'll show you where the Y is."

Billy Lee went back to work. He wrote in "Stock Clerk" for "Position Desired." He checked the boxes for both "Full-time Position" and "Part-time Position," just in case. He put down $125 a week as "Salary Desired," because he thought he could get by on that. He had only been making $40 a week in Crocketts.

By the time Billy Lee finished his application form, Howard had turned his in. Howard was waiting when Billy Lee came back from the counter himself.

"That wasn't so bad," said Billy Lee. "I thought job application forms would really be hard to fill out."

"That was an easy one," said Howard. "It was only one page long. And it didn't go into a lot of the things other job application forms do. The government says you can't ask certain questions on job application forms any more. But a lot of businesses still use old forms they have had for years. You didn't have any trouble on the last part, then?"

"Oh, I had to leave some blanks," said Billy Lee. "It's funny. I can't remember any of the telephone numbers of the people I've worked for. Some of the dates, too. Is that important?"

"It could be," said Howard. "It all depends on who is reading the forms. Come on. Let's go to the YMCA. We can talk about job application forms later."

CHAPTER 6
Rosalind

Billy Lee took a room at the Decatur YMCA. He looked up Rick Rodriguez soon after he moved in. That night, Rick and Billy Lee and Howard Plummer went out to dinner together. They went to Wa Fu's, a Chinese restaurant. Howard said you got a lot to eat there without spending a lot of money.

"This soup is really good!" said Billy Lee.

"You can ask for more if you want," said Howard.

"I don't want to get too full," said Billy Lee.

"I'll have some more," said Rick. He called to the waitress as she passed near their table. "Miss! I'd like some more soup, please."

The girl came to the table. "Would either of you like more soup?" she asked the other boys. She had a very nice smile.

"Not me," said Billy Lee.

"Nor I," answered Howard, going into his British West Indies accent. "But I must say, Miss, that it was a very good soup."

"Oh!" said the waitress. "You speak with a British accent. Where are you from?"

"I'm from the island of Marimba in the British West Indies," answered Howard. "And I note that you have a British accent too. Hong Kong?"

"Yes. I am from Hong Kong," answered the girl. "I have only lived in Chicago for six months."

"Did you come here to go to school?" asked Billy Lee.

The girl laughed. "No," she said. "I came here to work. My whole family came here to find work. But I must go now. We will talk later."

"People sure do come from all over to get jobs in Chicago," said Billy Lee.

"You have to go where there is work," said Howard. "Hong Kong is a very crowded place. It's even more crowded than Marimba."

"I've seen Hong Kong on TV," said Rick. "It's got more people crowded together than my neighborhood in Santo Christo."

"We don't get TV in Crocketts," said Billy Lee.

"No TV!" cried Rick. "I thought every place in America had TV."

"Well, lots of places don't," Billy Lee answered. "In Crocketts, the mountains block it out."

Soon the waitress was back with Rick's soup and the food they had ordered for dinner. She told them her name was Rosalind Chong. She said that she was working in Wa Fu's Restaurant only part-time. She was looking for a job in a store or in an office. Howard told her about the openings for salesclerks at Luderbach's Department Store. She was excited to hear about it.

The boys ate as much as they could. When they finished dinner, they began talking about what was on all their minds—jobs.

"I filled out my first job application form today," said Billy Lee to Rick. "It was no big thing. I can't understand why you have trouble with job application forms."

Rick didn't say anything.

Howard said, "That job application form was one of the easiest I have ever seen. Sometimes they are four pages long. But I'm pretty good at filling out job application forms now. If you have trouble filling one out, bring it to me, Rick. Some places will let you take an application form home with you."

"I have trouble understanding what they want," said Rick. "And even when I do understand, sometimes I don't know what to put down. And I can't print very well. They always want you to print when you fill one out. Look. I've got one with me that I picked up today. I usually just throw them away."

Rick took a job application form from his pocket. He gave it to Howard. Howard read it through. Then he said, "Tell you what, Rick. I'll help you fill this out later back at the Y. I think with some practice you won't have so much trouble filling out forms."

"I have to ask you something, Howard," said Billy Lee. "If you're so good at filling out forms, why haven't you been able to get a job?"

"I really don't know for sure," said Howard. "But maybe it's because I've got a record.

"A record of what?" asked Billy Lee.

"It's not a record *of*," said Howard. "It's a record *for*. For shoplifting. I was only 13 years old. But I was running with a bad crowd. I got caught first time out. They didn't put me away for it. But it's on my record just the same."

"And you think that's why you don't get hired?" asked Billy Lee. "Because you put that down on job application forms?"

"I can't be sure," answered Howard. "Some people may not want to hire me because I haven't had very much experience."

"Do you get a personal interview for any of the jobs you fill out applications for?" asked Billy Lee.

"Not when they ask about convictions on the forms," said Howard. "But some job application forms don't have questions like that. I've had interviews then sometimes."

"It doesn't seem fair," said Billy Lee. "After all, you were only 13 when you had that trouble. I think that if someone met you and talked to you, your record wouldn't mean a thing."

Howard smiled. "Thank you, Billy Lee," he said.

"But you have to answer a question like that honestly," said Rick. "They can find out if you have had a conviction. They would fire you from the job later when they found out."

"There's got to be some way to get around it," said Billy Lee. "Can't you add something on the application form? Why not write in, 'Happened when I was 13. Will explain fully during interview.'"

"You may have something there," said Howard. He laughed. "Funny an old expert like me didn't think of that! I'll try it next time."

Rosalind Chong had come back with their bill. She heard just the last part of what they were saying. "I had trouble with job application forms when I first came to America," she said. "I had trouble remembering names and dates and things. Then I got help from my Aunt Connie. She told me how to be prepared to fill in all the blanks on job application forms. She showed me how to make a Personal Information Sheet."

"How do you make one?" asked Billy Lee.

"I'll show you mine," said Rosalind. "I'll be back in a minute. I keep one in my bag."

Rosalind came back with her Personal Information Sheet. She gave it to the boys to read.

"This is good," said Howard as he read. "I keep some of these things on a card in my wallet. But it's better to have everything written out like this when you need it."

"It would help me for sure," said Rick.

"Me too," said Billy Lee. "I'm going to make one for myself."

"Let's all make out Personal Information Sheets tonight," said Howard. "We can help each other. Say, why don't we do this whole job hunting business as a team? We

can help each other to find jobs. We can use the same newspaper to find jobs in the Help Wanted ads. One of us can go into places and bring back job application forms for the others. We can take turns calling places on the telephone asking about jobs, too. Let's go back to the Y and get started!''

"Hold on!" cried Rick. "We haven't opened our fortune cookies yet.'' He broke open his cookie and pulled out a small piece of paper. "Get this," he said. " 'It's a wise man who listens to his friends.' ''

Billy Lee opened his fortune cookie. "The sun shines brightest after the darkest night,'' he read.

Howard laughed. "These cookies sure know what they are talking about. Mine says, 'He who thinks he knows it all, has much to learn!' ''

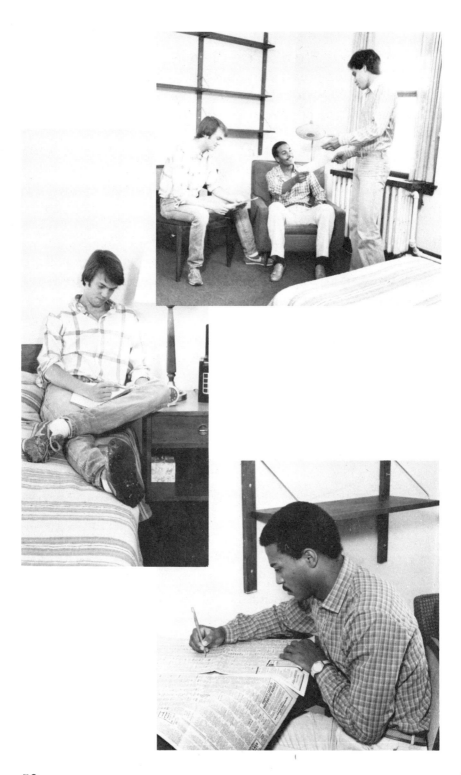

CHAPTER 7

Chicago—Our Home Town

Rosalind Chong let the three boys borrow her Personal Information Sheet. They began to work on their own Personal Information Sheets that night. They had finished them by the next night. In between, they made a plan to work as a team.

They decided to share the work this way. Howard would read the Help Wanted ads in the newspaper. He would circle each ad for a job that any one of them could apply for. He had the best telephone voice, so he would answer the ads that gave a telephone number. Billy Lee had the best handwriting. So he would answer all the ads that gave an address or a box number to write to. Rick would go to see about jobs for which you had to apply in person. And these were not only the jobs that were in the Help Wanted ads. He would call on any large business that hired a lot of people. When he went in to apply, he would also get job application forms for the other boys.

The three friends also decided to share the costs of job hunting. They would share the cost of newspapers, telephone calls, and transportation. And they would share the cost of stationery and stamps. They promised that they would continue helping each other until they all had jobs.

The plan got off to a good start. Howard Plummer got a job that week in the shipping department of Lyman-Harkus Department Store. He used Billy Lee's idea on the job application form this time. He checked the box saying that he had been convicted. But next to the box, he wrote that he had only been 13 years old at the time. "I can explain this fully during the interview," he added.

Howard told the job interviewer all about being convicted for shoplifting. He told her during the first few minutes of his personal interview. But he pointed out that he had never once been in trouble since that time. The interviewer liked Howard. He came across very open and honest to her. And she didn't think his record for shoplifting was all that important.

Rick Rodriguez practiced filling out job application forms every day. Howard and Billy Lee helped him. Soon he was able to print very well. And having a Personal Information Sheet made it easier every time he did it. By the end of the week, he was no longer afraid of job application forms.

Before the end of another week, Rick had two job offers. One job was with a building contractor as a helper. The other was an assembly-line job in a factory that made clocks. He picked the job with the contractor.

Billy Lee was getting discouraged. He was happy to see his friends get jobs. But he had been in Chicago almost three weeks, and his money was running out. Howard and Rick kept their promise and helped him as much as they could. And they offered him money when they got paid. But they could no longer share the work of looking for a job. Billy Lee was alone and unhappy most of the day.

He wished he knew why he hadn't been able to get a job. By now, he had filled out so many job application forms that he was an expert himself. He had job interviews, even tests, at some places. He just wasn't having any luck.

The day that Rick got his first pay, they all went to dinner again at Wa Fu's Restaurant. Rick and Howard were having a good time, but Billy Lee was not. "I guess I'll just have to go back to Crocketts," he said finally.

Howard looked sad. "I wish you wouldn't say that, Billy Lee," he said. "You know that Rick and I will help you. You'll get a job soon. You just have to hang in there. Don't break up the team now."

"I was just lucky to get something so fast," said Rick. "Look how long it took Howard to get a job. And he was an expert."

Rosalind Chong came to the table to take their order. She smiled and said hello. She asked them how their job hunting was going. They told her.

"I guess you didn't get a job at Luderbach's either," said Billy Lee.

"Not yet," said Rosalind. "I went down there the day after you told me about it. But it is still too soon to know. I asked the lady in the Personnel Department. She said that they sometimes don't call people in for interviews for a month or so. They like to have a lot of job applications all the time. In a big place like that, people are always leaving. They didn't really have any job openings for salesclerks when I went in. Many businesses do that. They take applications for jobs they expect to fill in the future."

"I didn't know that," said Billy Lee.

"I guess that's why we haven't heard from many of the places we applied at," said Howard.

"It figures," said Rick. "The employer has all the time in the world to find someone to fill a job. It's not like us, in a hurry to get a job."

"Oh, you can not be in a great hurry!" said Rosalind. "You can be lucky and get something quickly. But finding a job is usually something you must expect to take time.

That is the same all over. It was the same in Hong Kong. I know that. That is why I took a job here at Wa Fu's. It is better to have some work while you are looking for a job you like. And it is always easier to get a job if you are already working. Then an employer thinks that you are more worthy of hiring."

"Rosalind is right," said Howard. "Why don't you find a temporary job, Billy Lee? You know that place that has ads in the newspaper—Peoplepower? They send you out on jobs by the hour or by the day. Sign up with them and it will take care of some of your problems. You'll have money coming in. And that will give you time to wait until you hear from the employers you apply to."

Billy Lee smiled. It made sense to him. "All right," he said. "I'll go down there tomorrow."

"Now you're talking!" cried Howard. "And who knows, maybe your fortune cookie will tell you where to find a job tonight."

There were no surprises inside Billy Lee's fortune cookie. But his luck did begin to change. He got enough money from temporary jobs to pay his bills. He kept applying for jobs and filling out job application forms. Just about the time that he and Howard and Rick began looking for an apartment to share, he got several job offers.

Two offers were for jobs that he applied for weeks before—counter person at a fast-food restaurant and helper in a furniture store. One of them was for a job he applied for and was interviewed for on the same day. This was a job as an assistant to a veterinarian.

The veterinarian, Dr. Kaminski, had not seemed very interested in Billy Lee when he began to interview him. But then Billy Lee told him the story of why he had come to Chicago, and about his "interview" with Annie Grimes. The doctor could not stop laughing.

"I've never met Annie Grimes," Dr. Kaminski said finally. "But I believe every word of your story. Everyone in Chicago has heard about her. The old girl is certainly not all there. But she does like cats. How about you? Did your interview with the Cat Lady of Stockyard Boulevard turn you off cats?"

"Not at all!" said Billy Lee. "We have two cats at home. I like cats. I just didn't like the way she was keeping them. All that garbage! That's no way to keep animals."

"Well," said Dr. Kaminski, "you'll be happy to hear that the Health Department finally caught up with Annie. Closed her down for good. She went to live with her daughter in California."

"And all those cats?" asked Billy Lee.

"They will be taken care of," said the veterinarian. "They will go to good homes."

It was then that Dr. Kaminski offered Billy Lee the job. It was a good job with a future. It paid a higher salary than either Howard or Rick were making. And, if he wanted to go, Dr. Kaminski would help him to go to school for more training.

Billy Lee told Dr. Kaminski that he would take the job. Then Dr. Kaminski began to show him what he would be doing.

Billy Lee could hardly believe his good fortune. And to think he probably owed it all to Annie Grimes! He wouldn't even be in Chicago if it hadn't been for her. He was feeling very happy. It had been a very dark night. But the sun was shining brighter now than it ever had before.